All Is Well: Poems From the Detour

Monica Leigh Nelson

DEDICATION

For Grammy, who taught me about
the power of words and the love of God.

CONTENTS

ACKNOWLEDGMENTS

As with my first book, it would be impossible to list everyone who helped, but some must be mentioned. Again, I'd like to thank the nurses and oncologists at Dana-Farber Cancer Institute who helped me live to tell the tale. Carolyn Allard, who reads my rough drafts and makes them smoother. Any mistakes are clearly my own. My coworkers, caregivers, and faith family who read poem after poem and helped me decide which to add and which to lay aside. I would also like to thank all the members of the book club of the C.S. Lewis Society of Central Massachusetts who let me read my poems, and gave me honest feedback, and the Central Massachusetts Christian Writers Fellowship who encouraged me to keep writing.

As always, the greatest thanks goes to God, the co-author of my life.

DIAGNOSIS

SAVE THEM

"Save the tatas!"
somebody said.
But shouldn't we save
the women instead?

SOMETIMES

Sometimes we don't get to choose.
Sometimes God grabs our hands
and leads us on a journey.
One we may not understand.
One we would not have chosen.
But one that shapes,
        changes,
        or saves our life.
Because He is merciful.
Because He loves us.

CANCER

A heart-stopping
breath-stealing
speed bump
forcing you to hit the brakes,
slow down,
look around,
and change the direction of your life.

You take the detour.
five-year plans are postponed –
indefinitely –
as you wonder
what life will be like,
if life will be,
in five years.

It's funny –
the world really can
turn upside down
as friends step back and
strangers step forward.

The "unimportant"
becomes the most important.
                    Little wrapped trinkets.
            Eye contact.
            A song on the radio.
            Smiles in passing.
            The perfect shade of green.

Bills and deadlines
fade away.
No more rushing to get there.
Where you are is where you need to be.
No more self-improvement plans.
Who you are is who you need to be.
Just breathe.

Just live.

IN THE ARMS OF MY SHEPHERD

Thinking about the lump –
my nervousness,
my fears.
I talk about trust
and about You always being there.
But I'm still worried.
I'm afraid.

I pray
and listen
and wait.
I tell You I love You
and I picture myself
at Your feet,
gazing up into Your face.

I remember how the shepherd
reaches down to the sheep
and swings them up into His arms
against His heart.

And in my picture
of me at the feet of Jesus,
He reaches down
and swings me up
and holds me against His heart.
I am flooded
with the absolute knowledge
of His love
for me.

I am in the arms of my Shepherd.
All is well.

THE LONGEST DAYS

The longest days of my life
were those spent waiting
to see if I had cancer.

Part of me demanded
that I seize each moment,
honor every second,
laugh and live with friends and family,
not letting a single instant of time go unclaimed,
unappreciated,
unenjoyed.

But another part of me
just wanted to curl up into a ball
and rock,
lost in an if-only daydream,
waiting to wake up.
Waiting
for it all to go away.

But cancer doesn't just go away.

DIAGNOSIS DAY

You are awesome.
You are the Loving Creator God.
You are the One Who entered time
so that I may enter eternity.
You chose to feel pain
so that after we share my pain
I will know absence of pain.

How can I fear?
How can I doubt?
How can I curl up into myself and refuse to serve?
And, yet, somehow
I still do.

I'm sorry for that, Lord.

Let today just be more remodeling
as You use life to shape me,
cleanse me,
prepare me for Your use
and for Life.

Yes. Heaven is worth it.
All of it.
Anything Satan can throw at me –
anything You decide not to catch.
It's worth it.

To walk the streets of gold with my head up.
No fear, no shame, no worry
about what might happen to my son when I'm not looking.
Seeing You face to face,
collapsing at Your feet in joy and thankfulness.
Feeling Your touch.

Yes. It's worth it.

THE BATTLE

God never asks us to do something
we can't do –
in His strength.

Cancer is my job right now.
A job He's been preparing me for
my whole life.
And this
is just preparation
for something else.

And the staggering obvious
becomes clear again –
it's all part of His good, divine plan.

He had this in mind
when He introduced my mother to my father.
My grandmother to my grandfather.
Adam to Eve.

This was not a surprise attack by the enemy,
which God quickly found a way
to use to His advantage.

God knew this was coming all along,
and He's been preparing each of us for it.
For the role we'll each play in it.

This is part of the battle
to advance God's kingdom on earth.

And I have the easiest job of all.
Simply to stand.
To endure.
To be still –
and to shout the praises of the God
Who is winning this war.

INVITED

Cancer tried to sneak into my life,
    Derail my plans,
        Cripple my body,
            And devastate me.

But it didn't know that the Master
    Who walks on water,
        Who shrivels barren fig trees,
            Who teaches cells to grow and divide,
            Came here first.

So cancer came invited into my life,
    Refocused my plans,
        Strengthened my body,
            And encouraged me
                To trust the Master with each breath,
                  With each heart beat,
                    With my very existence.

THE "C" WORD

Christ.
He created me.
He cherishes me.
He called, chased, and caught me.
He cleansed me.
He cares for me.
And He will carry me through.

IT'S FUNNY…

It's funny the odd moments I think of it.
Like when I turn off the computer
and stand up
and the words flash through my mind,
"I have cancer."

I don't cry.
I'm not upset.
It's just odd.

How could it possibly be true –
when I can still do such mundane things
as watch a home movie of my son's band concert
or play two rounds of spider solitaire?

My life is so normal.
How could it possibly be true?
And the thought moves on.

And yet, I'm changed.
Because I know it is true.
And now,
deep down beyond the level of words,
I know that there really is no mundane.

Anyone can get cancer.
Absolutely anyone.

Even me.

NO OTHER WAY

I have a student.
A second grader.
A boy who loves reading books, is good at math, works slowly,
but gets everything done and done well.
A student who's going to a wake tomorrow.
For his father.

Cancer struck again.

And for this moment, it really feels like cancer won.
For this moment, cancer is Huge. Horrible.
Terrifying and Powerful.
It's Merciless – taking the father of a seven-year-old boy.
A boy who always did his homework.
Who kept his desk neat.
Who never forgot to say "Please" and "Thank you"
and was always willing to help.

And now I clench my fists and shout up to Heaven –
"Why? Why, Abba? Why? What good is there in this? Why?"

It's a touch of survivor's guilt, a dash of fear,
a sprinkle of hopelessness, and a whole bunch of anger.
I'm angry
At cancer.
At Satan.
And I think I'm finally angry at God.
Surely there must have been another way.

But there couldn't have been.
Because my Abba doesn't make mistakes.
He doesn't.
He hasn't.
He never will.

He's all powerful, tempered by mercy and love.
He holds me tightly, even when I'm beating on His chest.
Because He loves me.
And He loves that little boy.

Cancer sucks.

I hate it.
I hate what it did to me.
To my family.
To my coworkers.
To my students.
But somehow, in some way,
it too is a tool in my Master's hand.
Somehow, even this, can point to You.

I can almost picture those streets of gold.
I can almost hear the children's laughter and singing
as they play in that golden alley.
I can almost taste the salty tears of joy
that will be flowing down my face.

God is still in control, and this too shall pass.
This, too.
Hold that boy's hand, Lord.
Let this take him on a journey that ends in Your arms.
Keep his heart soft.
Guide him through this pain.
Get him through tomorrow.

JOY FOR FEAR

I'm scared today.
So much ahead.
So much sickness.
The journey is too much for me.

But You've made this path for me.
Help me to walk it willingly.
Give me the grace
for each moment
You bring me to.

Hold my shaking heart.
Send Your comfort.
Help me be a comfort
to the hurting around me
instead of just dwelling on myself.

Take my fear
and give me Your joy.

YOU ARE GOOD

You are a God of miracles.
You created the world and the universe.
And You created me.

I know You are perfectly capable of preventing cancer.

And I believe
beyond a shadow of a doubt
that You love me.

You do miracles for me.
You care about the little details of my life.
You want my good.
You love my laughter.

So,
somehow,
this is for my good.

Maybe something amazing will happen – later.
Maybe good will come of me simply having cancer.

I don't know.
But You do.
You are omnipotent.
And You love me infinitely.

So I will trust.

I will wait and see.

And while I'm waiting,
I will taste and see
how good You are.

TREATMENT

PSALM 46:1-3

Let the chemo steal my strength.
Let the Taxol steal my breath.
Let the nausea come during the night.
God is my refuge
and holds me in the palm of His hand.
I will not fear the cancer
or its treatment.

A BRIEF REBELLION

Like a stubborn two year old,
I cross my arms and stamp my feet,
glaring at God and shouting, "No!" into eternity.

Then my face crumples,
my lower lip trembles,
and my arms unfold
as I fly forward into my Abba's arms
                                    and weep
                          and weep
                          and weep.

"I want to have breasts."
                    "I know."
"I don't want to lose my hair."
                    "I know."
"I'm scared."
                    "I know."
"I'm overwhelmed. It's too much!"
                    "I know."
"I can't do it."
                    "I can."

And He holds me as I cry.

There's no warmer place
than wrapped in my Abba's arms.
Oh – to stay here forever.
Safe.
Cherished.
Untouched by the woes of the world.

Hair and breasts are unimportant in my Abba's arms.
Tears are unneeded.
Time doesn't exist.
Pain doesn't matter.

My Abba's arms protect me,
support me, and then so slowly
        – but way too quickly –

release me.

I cannot live in my Abba's arms.
Not yet.

With a gentle nudge,
I'm back in the world.
But it looks different.
It feels different.

The tears are dried up.

And suddenly there's hope in my heart
and (is it possible?) joy!

"Did I do it?"
Suddenly, I'm a proud second grader,
hopping on one leg
with the other foot behind my knee
looking up for affirmation.
"Did I pass?"
>   "*Yes.*" God chuckles back.
>   "*Yes — you passed.*"

And I feel the gentle squeeze
of a hand on my shoulder,
the warmth of an arm behind my bare neck.
When He pushed me back into the world,
my Abba never let me go.
And I will never give up.

BRAVE WORDS

My story can't end after only one chemo treatment.
I will not give up here or now.
I want to live to dance and tell the world
of the joy found only in You.

Not despite the pain,
but in the midst of the pain.
Because of the pain.
You are bigger than my cancer.
My cancer couldn't move into my lymph nodes
without first going through You.
And if You said yes for some heavenly reason,
I can say yes, too.

Brave words.
But I'm still scared…

I have the feeling we'll be taking this same journey
over and over again.
        "As many trips as you need, My child.
        Just keep coming back to me."
You really do love me, don't You, Lord?
        "Yes."

I feel Your warmth,
soft against my irritated, sensitive skin.
My God loves me.
There is still so much out there to be afraid of.
But my God loves me.
I can cling to that.

A LOW

This is one of my low points, I guess.
One of those moments
when you can have faith
and say, "Yes, Lord. I trust You.
        My life is in Your hands.
        You'll take good care of me."

But your hands aren't being held.
Your forehead isn't being kissed.
No one's arms are going around your shoulders.

As the memories of other lonely sobbings come,
today's tears dry.
I've been lower.

And each time, in time,
God lifted me back up.
This, too, shall pass.
I'm where I'm supposed to be,
and God has told me He loves me
very clearly.
So many times.

I'm sorry, Lord, for letting my focus
slide down with my emotions.
I choose to trust, and wait.

TODAY

Today, I don't like cancer.
At all.
Today, I'm angry.
At the little deformed cells that just refuse to die.
And perhaps,
a little,
at the God Who could have made them follow the rules.

Today, I'm frustrated
at all the things I can do nothing about.
I can't add an inch to my hair.
I can't keep people from dying.
I can't protect the people I love
from my pain.

And today, I'm tired.

But I guess I'm allowed to have bad days, too.
I'm allowed to get a bit angry
and to turn to God and wonder why.

He just wants me to turn to Him.

So I will.
When I'm looking at Him,
instead of at me,
or even at the world around me –
that's when my heart begins to believe
that this might actually turn out okay.

JUST AROUND THE CORNER

Abba – I can't do this without You.
Be near to me.
Be real to me.
Help me.
Heal me.
Take me. I'm Yours.
I love You, Lord. Very much.
Thank You for what You've done for me.
Thank You for Your unfailing
unfathomable
faithfulness.
I will remember.
I will write it on my hands.
I will hang it on my walls.
I will burn it into my memory.
You are faithful.
This is temporary!
I am on a journey, ever becoming
more You-like.
You have done so much.
Jesus loves me
and Jesus lives.
I will not forget.
I will not dwell on my disappointments.
On the plans I made that had to be let go.
Instead, I will dwell on Your love
and the plans that You've made –
incredibly perfect plans – for me –
just around the corner.
Lord, I am waiting.
Waiting on Your promises.

IT'S OKAY

It's okay if I can't make the pieces fit in the puzzle.
It's okay if I can't always hold myself together –
never mind the world around me.

It's okay if I just don't feel like bending down
to pick that piece of lint off the rug.
It's okay if I didn't get a chance to iron my blouse,
wash the dinner dishes,
or feed the fish.
Just this once.

It's okay if my hair is straight, or curly, or even frizzy.
It's okay if I need to call in sick,
or call out for supper.
Or call up for help.

It's okay if I'm not superwoman.
Or supermom.
Or even super special.

Sometimes I'm just okay.
And that's okay.

A SURGERY-EVE GIFT

A stressed-out
surgery eve.
A walk to a tavern
for a last supper.
Across the parking lot,
a convenience store,
so we stop
to hunt for chocolate.

A tall black man,
heavily accented,
totaling costs
and making change
and small talk.

"Why are you in Boston?"
"I have surgery tomorrow."
"You have surgery?"
"Yes."
"I give you peace."

A sincere "Please come back"
as the bell chimed
over the door.

Eating chocolate,
reentering the hotel.
Now smiling
instead of worrying
about the morning.

THE MIRROR

I'm a mess.
And I'm allowed to be.

Today, I looked in the mirror
and told my reflection,
"I don't know you."
Then my eyes filled with tears
as I whispered,
"And I don't want to."

Because I don't.

I don't want to get to know
this fearful person
with short curly hair
and a chest full of scars.
I don't want her to be me.

But she is.
That's who I've become.

After years of digging and learning,
I'd finally discovered the me I wanted to be.
And it only took 15 months of chemo,
radiation, and surgery
to take it all away.

It's time to start over.

But I don't want to.
It's easier to run through each day
grading papers, watching movies,
reading books, making plans –
I don't have time
to face myself in the mirror.

Who really does that anyway?

A TIME TO CRY

I sobbed in Abba's arms tonight
because the world is so heavy
and I am so small.
Too small
to carry all of the hopes
and hurts
I've jammed into my heart.
Jumbled thoughts of fear and sorrow
tumbling over the bits of laughter.
grief anger loss pain
The burden's too great.
The world's too heavy
tonight.

Abba's tears mingle with my own.
He rocks me
as He gently whispers,
"Hope."
"This too shall pass."
"Rest. For the journey is too much for you."
My Abba holds me
as I close my eyes
and the tears turn to sleep
in peace.

I am small.
But He is huge.
My Abba holds the world.
All will be well.

SO SIMPLE

Is it really so simple?
Can I really just reach out,
take Your hand,
and go to the mountaintop
at any time?

Can all of this
really become meaningless?
Do You really cry with me
over the aches and pains
and regretful losses?

Sometimes,
when life goes on,
when the mundane keeps needing doing,
and the surgeons and oncologists keep saying,
"One more,"
it seems
You might not really care.
You're not doing anything.

But I guess that's because
You're not in the doing.
Everything that's truly important
has already been done.

So I'll sit
still
reaching out to take Your hand.

ALL IS WELL

"Abba, am I going to die?"

> *"Yes, My child."* You softly whisper.
> *"All mortal ones do.*
> *Even my Beloved Son.*
> *But don't worry about the how or the when.*
> *It's all in My hands.*
> *You are in My hands."*

"Oh, Abba, I don't want to do this."

> *"I know."*

"I'm scared."

> *"I know."*
> Gentle. Loving. Confident.
> His voice brings assurance and reassurance.
> *"This too shall pass.*
> *My grace is sufficient.*
> *Come to me and rest a while when the journey is too much.*
> *I love you."*

I realize that I'm not as tired as I'd thought.
I'm weary, bruised, and broken.
I'm ready to give in, but not to give up.
My God is bigger than my cancer.
My life will go on.

"Thank You, Father. Just for being You."

> *"You're welcome, Child."*

I feel His smile like a hug.
God is in control.
All is well with my world.

PICKING UP
THE PIECES

MOVING THE MOUNTAIN

I'm trying to move my mountain
with my own big, heavy shovel.
And God just watches and waits.

Finally, desperately, shamefacedly,
I hand over my heavy shovel.
"Here, God.
You move my mountain."

He grins as He balances my huge shovel
on the tip of His little finger.
It's smaller than His fingernail.
I grin back at Him.
That shovel was way too small to move a mountain.

Then He smiles at me,
turns to my mountain
and gently puffs.
Like blowing out a candle,
or blowing a kiss.

The mountain flew off into the breeze
like millions of bits of dust.
And suddenly it was gone.
Only God remained,
at my side,
with a useless shovel balanced on His finger.

"Trust me, Little One.
I can move mountains."

NOW WHAT?

Only bits and pieces,
just broken segments,
are left of my old life.
The word "normal"
has become
completely meaningless.

It's like
climbing up the stairs
after a tornado.
So grateful to be alive,
but so shell-shocked
by the utter chaos
all around you.

Where do you start?
What do you do first?
How do you learn
to live with the knowledge
that disaster struck here?
With the fear
that it might be back?

I survived
by the skin of my teeth.

Now what?

WAKING UP

I feel like
I'm very slowly waking up from a deep sleep
only to discover
that the world
aged
while I was asleep.

Like I'd gone away for a few years
and came back to discover
that everything had changed while I was gone.
Drastically.

I'm stepping off the moving sidewalk.
I'm preparing to exit the VIP lounge of the cancer club.

I know the world is different.
I know that my relationships with my friends are different.
I know that I am different.

And I'm petrified.

Oh – but I'm stubborn.
And I'm strong.
I'm a survivor.

I AM ALIVE

Sometimes,
when it's quiet,
I still wonder,
"Is it back?"

But that first diagnosis day
was so long ago
that I almost never think of it anymore.

Now my first thought,
when I feel a new ache or pain,
is, "Ugh! I'm getting old."

There was a time
when I thought that
would never happen to me.

But those bald chemo days,
those blistered radiation days,
those wheeled-in-to-surgery days
are far enough away
to have let the fears fade with the scars.

I am alive –
and that thought
is no longer a whisper of shock,
or a shout of defiance.
It's merely a statement of fact.

I now crawl into bed
fully expecting
to wake up in the morning.
Taking each minute for granted
as if I'll never run out.

Until,
abruptly,
my heart remembers.

A strand of hair between my fingers,

a glass of juice the color of a chemo,
a glimpse of a scar.
And I begin to wonder,
"Is it back?"

But my heart keeps beating.
The rest of the hair stays on my head.
The juice is just juice.

And I am alive.
Right now.
Right where I am.
Alive.

And I can live with that.

WHO AM I?

I'm just wondering –
who am I?
I think I'm still me.
But I'm not the same me.

I'm a very tired me.
When I'm out having fun,
I often suddenly realize that it isn't fun anymore
and I have to drag myself home
and crawl into bed exhausted.
There are so many things I don't get to.
There's so much I leave undone.

I think I'm a more serious me.
Or maybe a less serious one.
When people get caught up
in heated arguments and debates
that used to thrill me,
my mind quickly wanders away
to things that now matter more.
Intellectual discussions don't grip my thoughts
as tightly as they used to.
I really don't care
if the latest author agrees with the latest opinions.
I'd rather be talking about –
about what?
About me?
About cancer?
About the repercussions
of a life with no breasts in American society?

Actually,
lately,
I haven't really joined the discussions at all.
I just sit there,
occasionally smiling,
trying to care,
but still zoning out.

Maybe it's the chemo brain.
Or the fatigue.

Maybe it's post-traumatic stress syndrome.
Or maybe it's just the new me.

But who is that?
And how do I get to know her?
That's the journey I'm on.
A journey that right now
seems to be as daunting
as Frodo's with the ring.

How do you get to know the person
who lives in your skin?
How do you become acquaintances,
and then friends,
with the stranger in the mirror?
How do you go through the stages
of grieving for the person you used to be
before the process of healing
tore your world apart?

How do you get up
each morning
and go about the motions of daily life
when you don't even know who you are?

I suppose it's like any great journey.
You start
by stepping forward.

A TRIBUTE TO THE ONE

You are the One Who made me.
You are the One Who allowed my cancer cells to divide and grow.
You are the One Who planted wisdom in my oncologist.
The One Who counted the hairs on my head
as they fell out, then grew back in.

You made the chemo curl my hair and turn my reds to grays.
You allowed the radiation to brown and blister my skin
and search and destroy any remaining cancer cells
like hungry little Pacmen.
You made my scars heal flat.

You determined the days of my life and decreed they weren't over yet.
You chose for me to survive.

You are the Creator of sunshine.
Of every star that shines.
You are the Father of the Son
Who accepted the whips and nails on my behalf.
You are the Great Teacher
Who showed the waters how to flow downhill
and taught the oceans how to ebb under the pull of the moon.

You made ants who can lift so much more than they are.
You made flowers whose only purpose
is to sway in the breeze and look indescribably beautiful.
You made the winds that can lift houses without even being seen,
that can move in any and every direction at once.
That can die without a moment's warning.

And then You made me.

You placed me in a home with a mom and a dad and a big brother.
And You never left my side as I grew.
As I traveled around the world.
As I learned and laughed.
As I cried at loss and in confusion.
As I felt pain and wondered why.
As I found You and found joy and so-peaceful contentment.
As I danced at the tasks You placed before me.
As I daily discovered anew who You were making me to be.

As I became a mom, and a teacher, and an aunt.

And You were still there as I placed my all in Your hands
and followed the advice of my oncologists
and survived.

And You will still be there all the rest of my days
as I continue to survive.
As I learn to dance again.
As I learn to live with the always-fear of a recurrence,
of a death,
around the next corner.

You are here.

LOOKING GOOD

People say how good I look.
How strong I am.
How well I'm doing.
They talk about how cute my hair looks,
and how beautiful my smile is.
They talk about me being hope,
an inspiration. An example.
Then they go home and finish living their own lives.

And I'm left here
with the shredded remains of my life,
without an inkling
of how to put the pieces back together.
Without even an inkling of who I am,
of who I've become.

I don't even have the oddly comforting protection
of looking sick anymore.
I don't have the chemo nausea and side effects
to hide behind anymore.
I just have a bunch of scars over a broken heart.
All the dreams I've had to let go.
All the hopes and plans
that got ripped out of my hands.

I know this is just a down moment.
That it'll pass.
That in the morning
I'll be bathed in Your joy again.
But right now, I'm sad.

I'm sad that I no longer have breasts.
I'm sad that I feel so alone.
That I'm lying here crying into a pillow
and writing these words into a notebook
instead of being able to tell them to a friend.

Because my friends just say how good I look.
How well I'm doing.
That I'm such an inspiration.

POSSIBILITIES

"Possibilities."
It's no longer a Pollyanna piping,
but a dreadful whisper
of what could be.

Every ache and twitch
is cancer's cry,
"Don't get comfortable. I might be back."

"Peace!"
cries the Master
Who controls the wind and the waves.

And at His sure voice
I see through the haze

Possibilities
of a life cancer free

THE GOD OF RIPPLES

Sometimes I'm still fearful that the cancer will sneak back.

I imagine it slipping into the lymph nodes
or sinking like a pebble in the center of my brain
with the ever widening ripples changing life as I know it
into a nightmare.
My heart pounds.
My eyes begin to water.
What if?

But then my Abba reminds me
that He is the God of ponds, rocks, and ripples,
as well as little cells,
and my heart knows again that all is well.

Come whatever may,
I am in my Father's hands.

Hands that hang the pine needles on the evergreens.
Hands that help the great white shark give birth.
Hands that press a piece of coal into a diamond.
Hands that keep the planets aligned.
Hands that can write on stones, scribble in sand,
and corral errant cancer cells.

Those hands are holding me.

A MOMENT

Hold my heart for a moment.
Keep me in peace –
just for a moment.

Then later You can put me back in the world
ready to serve You.
Ready to get back to the journey.

Later.

Right now, let me rest in Your arms.

You really are bigger than my cancer, aren't You?
Than anyone's cancer.

Let me cling to Your Love, Peace, Goodness, Safety –
just for another moment.
Then I'll continue the journey.

It never ends, does it?
My cancer journey.
I'm going to be on it for the rest of my life.

THE PANIC

I cried today.
I thought about the 17th of May
and found it hard to breath.
I was petrified.

But of what?
Of cancer?
Of dying?
Of recurrence,
and having to do chemo again?

I don't know.
I don't even know what I'm scared of.

Abba, hold my heart,
just as You have my whole life.
Through each trauma.
Each scary moment.

You were with me each time I cried.
You sat beside me in every doctor's office.

I am not alone.
I'm in Your arms.

This painful panic is not forever.
Only You are.

This will pass.
I will be dancing in Your joy again one day.

Until then,
Your grace is sufficient.
I choose to trust You.

I will survive.

A CLOSED BOOK

It's amazing
how so much misery
fear
and pain
can fit into a box of mementos,
a simple scrapbook,
and be so almost completely forgotten.
We close the book
and move on,
rarely looking back.

It's equally amazing
how quickly
and vividly
it all rushes back
when a wandering finger
brushes across a new lump.

Your heart stops beating.
Your lungs can't take in air.
Your pores start pouring out
cold, sticky sweat.
"I trust my Abba for every breath"
instantly becomes,
"I'm going to die."

Then family and friends
draw alongside.
Questions are answered.
A forgotten God
reasserts His omnipotent presence.
Bumps become scar tissue.
Fears are reassured.

Another book swings closed
and life moves on again.

THANK YOU

JOY

There's a joy in my heart.
Through You. In You. Because of You.
Complete, mind-blowing, body-tingling,
stabilizing joy.
One of Your many, many gifts to me.
A joy that doesn't depend on circumstances,
that doesn't depend on people,
that doesn't depend on what mood I'm in,
what clothes I'm wearing,
what day it is.
A joy that only depends on You.
A joy that warms my heart in snowstorms,
comforts my heart in chaos,
and cradles my heart snuggly
when the world is lost and confused around me.
A joy that is faithful,
enduring,
trustworthy, and endearing.
A joy that can be spread from heart to heart,
smile to smile,
soul to soul,
at the whisper of Your name,
in the reading of Your word.
A joy that is more powerful than the life around me,
that can smile through tears,
that can hug through hate,
that can hold on when everyone else lets go.
A joy beyond understanding,
beyond comprehension,
beyond my wildest dreams,
but not beyond my reach –
because You've placed it within my heart.

LIFE MOVES FORWARD

I'm not who I was
and I never will be again.
Things will never go back
to how they used to be.

Life moves forward.

But life
doesn't simply "go on"
after cancer.
It can still be enjoyed.

I can still laugh.
I can still feel the joy of success.
I can still
dance in the rain,
read books in the sun,
cuddle with kittens,
and watch flowers sway in the wind.

The new me
can have
just as much fun
as the old me.

Life is good.

Life is still good.

LIFE

Five years ago, I got the cold news
And I had to accept that we don't get to choose
Our life.

As I let go of my hair, and both my breasts, too,
I found all the things I still had to cling to –
Like life.

The love of my Savior, the faith of my son,
The hope of my friends, your cards by the ton
Filled life.

These five years went by in a laughter-filled daze
With milestones – like this one – shining bright in the haze
Of life.

Now I have new breasts, and soft curly hair.
Plus the calming assurance that you will always be there
Through life.

Thank you again – for all wearing pink.
For once more pointing out that there's more than I think
To life.

It's sunshine and smiles and pink butterflies.
The love of a friend and homemade whoopee pies
Make life.

Because of your strength, I can stand tall.
And when you're beside me, it's okay to fall
In life.

Whatever comes next – if I laugh or I sigh –
I'm so grateful that you are a glad part of my
Life.

YOUR FIGHT

My cancer diagnosis
Shattered a lot of hearts.
    The world stopped.
    The worries started.
Why? What if? Why didn't? If only… No way.

Some people just ran.
It wasn't their fight.
    They didn't stop to call
    or find time to write.
Some of my friends just faded away…

Some people baked meals.
A lot sent cool cards
    (or strawberries and pjs)
    with love, prayer, and regards.
The help and the laughter brightened each day.

And some took a stand
Right next to me.
    Some days they'd listen.
    Some days they'd lead.
Their gentle wisdom would point out my way.

This was your battle.
It wasn't just mine.
    You fought when I couldn't
    and you let me whine.
You got me through cancer and all I can say

Is thank you

FIFTY CARDS

A tumor snuck in like a thief in the night.
It whisked away my peace, left me with fright.

Frozen, I panic. Who knows what'll come next.
My dreams are all shattered. My future is hexed.

I stare at my battle scars. I touch my short hair.
I feel pain in places that are no longer there.

The darkness is darker than my worst nightmares thought,
and the sun doesn't shine on my dark little spot.

What about me? Have I been forgotten?
Sitting home alone, taking my Dilotin.

But each day, like clockwork, the mailman shows up
with envelopes with my name scrolled across the top.

Some are big, thick, and bulgy
with kind thoughts and prayers.
Some are full of advice or leave glitter everywhere.

Some make jokes, some tell stories,
some just want to remind me
that I am never alone, that the sun still shines brightly.

Each card is a brick in the new life I'm making.
Each sender a signpost on the journey I'm taking.

The signs that they're holding?
"Hope." "Trust." "Keep on going."
"Your future is beautiful." "Your hair's really growing."

So dear friends, I thank you for the daily reminders
that joy can come down to fifty cards in a binder.

I am not forgotten. My dreams are not shattered.
The cancer didn't really take anything that mattered.

I still have you, and God still has me.
I'm letting go of despair to step forward, free.

CHRISTMAS CHILD

A Christmas child, a cancer cell.
Two different stories, but both tell
of a loving God and His odd-seeming gifts
full of both tears and Spirit lifts.

Who'd have thought that a baby boy
two thousand years later would still bring joy?
And who'd have thought that a cancer cell
could grow and divide and cause such a swell

of friendship and kindness and closeness and trust.
The new laughter alone is worth the new bust.
The friends that I've gathered, the family I found
placed my wandering feet on firm, settled ground.

God's gifts are good, though oft strangely clad –
like a poorly formed cell or a carpenter's lad.
Thank you for letting my God use you
to gently remind me He is Faithful and True.

Thank you for being a part of my Hope.
To use a cliché, you're the knot on my rope.
Remember this New Year all that God has done.
The gift of my cancer, the gift of His Son,

the gift of forgiveness,
the gift of good friends,
and the Promise of Heaven –
where all pain will end.

THANK YOU

Dear Father,
Thank You for being bigger than the achy days.
Thank You for loving me in such simple ways.

Kibble in the cat bowl,
Freshly baked food,
Soft blankets and tissues,
A calm, peaceful mood.
Sunsets and rainbows,
Milk in my jar,
Smooth satin pillows,
And gas in my car.
Laughter at work,
Little hands in my own,
An almost clean room,
A just-found cell phone.
Sunshine and snowdrops,
Fresh starts every day.
People beside me
Each step of the way.

I'm a survivor because You hold my heart.
In the light, in the dark,
Lord, how great Thou art!

A TASTE

Abba –
      Thank You.

Thank You for the Detour.
      For the bumps in the road.
      For the players who joined my team
          and cheered me on.
For Your presence – in the MRI tubes,
             In the operating rooms,
             In the middle of the night.

For five years.

Thank You for stepping into time to walk with me.
      For giving my heart a taste of the glories
      I will drink deeply of in Heaven.

Thank You for the pearls we find in our pain.

WITHOUT GOD

I can't imagine
if there were no God.
If life really were
just a string of random events
with no Master Designer
controlling the catastrophes.

With no Hope of anything else –
when you stop breathing on earth
you no longer exist.
When loved ones stop breathing,
they no longer exist.

How do you survive the panic?
Every breath you inhale
could be your very last one.
How do you bear the present sorrow
without the certainty of future joy?

What would be the point of honor,
of sacrifice, of love, and selflessness?

How do people manage
their day-to-day existence
in such darkness?

How do you defeat cancer –
an insidious, silent, inhuman assassin –
without God?

Thank God we don't have to.
Thank God He is real.
My comfort. My company.
He is my answer.

He walked this world
until His body gave out.
He was sad, scared, and alone.
He created the bridge
to a world without despair or loneliness.
He is that bridge.

ACKNOWLEDGMENT

I had cancer.
One little cell
divided and multiplied and refused to die.
It split
and grew
and split again
and grew again
until it became a lump
in the upper left of my chest.
The cells overflowed the ducts
into the breast tissue,
then squeezed into the lymph nodes
where they began plotting
where to travel next.

Then I endured chemo.
A port was surgically placed in my chest,
connected to my jugular,
leaving another lump
and an inch long scar.
Poison was pumped into my body
making me horribly nauseous.
My hair fell out.
My ovaries stopped functioning.
My body grew weak
and confused.

But the cancer cells began to die.

I had surgeries.
One
after another
after another
until I lost count.
Biopsies leaving scattered scars.
Bilateral mastectomies
that removed my breasts
and replaced them
with scars and pain.
Some visible,

some hidden deep in my heart.

But the cancer cells were removed.

I had 36 days of radiation.
Gentle and simple at first.
Then tingling.
Then burning.
Then oozing blistered skin.

But any remaining cancer cells were neutralized.

I had reconstructive surgery.
Surgeries.
Expanders.
Implants.
Muscles converted to pockets.
Fat grafts.
"Almost done."
"Just one more."
"We're as close as we can get."
"We're done."

But the cancer didn't win.

MEET ME

I put a bowl on the floor this morning,
and watched my cat lick it.
A noisy bit of my mind was urging,
"Do something.
Wash dishes. Wipe the counter. Sweep the floor.
Do something."
Then I realized,
"I am. I'm watching my cat. I'm being."
That's just as important.
Being is just as good as doing.

Abba taught me that.
Just as He taught me to be comfortable
in my own skin again.
And to love being me.

I don't have real breasts.
But I've got new bumps.
My hair is long; and I smile quickly.
I love games and nature walks.
I endure cleaning because I like a picked-up house,
but I'd much rather be reading books.
I'm not a great cook,
but I can pull together a yummy meal.
I eat way too much chocolate,
but I nibble on carrot sticks, too.
My car is paid off,
and I might get a bike.
I've got a tan
and a closet full of clothes,
and most of them fit.
I'm not afraid of death anymore –
I know where I'm going.
And after four solo road trips
I've found I'm good company.

Thank You, Abba,
for the places You've brought me on this journey.
Thank You for introducing me to Me.

COME WHATEVER MAY

The cancer in remission –
or the cancer that comes back.
The friends who'll walk beside me
to a mansion, or a shack.
Through all the ups and downs
over twisty, unmarked roads
Your grace will keep me standing
and You'll never let me go.

You know my joy and sorrow.
You allow each sinking pain.
It breaks Your heart to see me cry,
so I glorify Your name.
For each hurt just brings me closer
to who You meant me to be.
Little pieces of a puzzle
that we can't yet fully see.

You are my creator.
You formed my heart and soul.
And then You made a path for me
with Heaven as my goal.

Abba – thank You for the sunlight,
and thank You for the clouds.
Thank You for Your whispers,
and my joyous shouts out loud.
Thank You for forgiveness –
each day a brand-new start.
Thank You for Your healing,
and for sheltering my heart.

Come whatever may,
I will choose to trust in You,
clinging to Your saving grace
til my last day is through.

ABOUT THE AUTHOR

Monica Nelson is an elementary school teacher and a seven-year cancer survivor currently living in Charlton, Massachusetts. A former missionary kid, she writes devotionals and praise poetry, as well as gently humorous essays and poems about cancer treatments and their side effects. She also posts frequent anecdotes about Stella and Wyatt, her rescue cats, and Wesley, her twenty-year-old son.

Printed in Great Britain
by Amazon

86293758R00041